THE KEY TO ART

THE KEY TO ART
FROM ROMANTICISM TO IMPRESSIONISM

A Bateman/Search Press Pocket Guide

Carlos Reyero
Professor of Art History

Search Press, Tunbridge Wells, England
in association with
David Bateman, Auckland, New Zealand

The publisher wishes to thank Dale Haworth, Professor of
Art History, Carlton College, for his assistance in the
preparation of this book.

First published in Great Britain 1990
Search Press Limited
Wellwood, North Farm Road
Tunbridge Wells, Kent, TN2 3DR

In association with David Bateman Ltd.
32-34 View Road, Glenfield, Auckland, New Zealand

ISBN 0-85532-667-0

A David Bateman Book

Printed in Spain

INTRODUCTION

Evaluation, Tendencies, and Terminology

The idea that no distinct artistic style emerged during the 19th century was a common belief during that period and one that still persists today. Although it is true that most artistic forms used during the 19th century are no different from those of other periods, the words *19th century* do have a meaning that is much wider than a mere reference to time.

CHARLES GARNIER. Great Stairway at the Opera. 1860-64. Paris. The Opera in Paris is an important work that typifies the architecture of the 19th century. The building is an outstanding example of the architecture of the Second Empire. Perfectly situated on its surrounding square of land, it was a point of reference for Parisian town planning. It has all of the elements of Eclectic Classicism, and its sumptuous interior shows the taste of the powerful middle class for the grandiose and overpowering. Because of its luxurious and exaggerated detail, it has an unequalled capacity to surprise.

MAP

Paris is considered to have been the most important artistic centre of the 19th century. It was receptive to new ideas and served as a reference point for the rest of Europe in all art forms throughout the century. But there were also other artistic centres where new ideas sprang up before or at the same time as those in France. Classical art influenced much 19th-century art. Rome (which is known for its Classical art) exercised an artistic power over cities such as Paris and Venice. Important 19th-century art was also created in London, Berlin, Vienna, Munich, Budapest, Brussels, as well as the artistic centres of Russia, Spain, and Portugal. Eventually, art was no longer exclusively European: The United States started producing its own art, which, in turn, had some influence on Europe. Nineteenth-century European art was also influenced, stylistically and iconographically, by cultures from the Near and Far East.

1. St. Petersburg
2. Berlin
3. Dresden
4. Vienna
5. Munich
6. Copenhagen
7. Venice
8. Florence
9. Rome
10. Barcelona
11. Madrid
12. Lisbon
13. Paris
14. London
15. Brussels

In some way, the words *19th century* serve to unify what some art historians have tried very hard to put into categories. These historians are referring to artistic tendencies whose development can be traced from the end of the 18th century to the end of the 19th century.

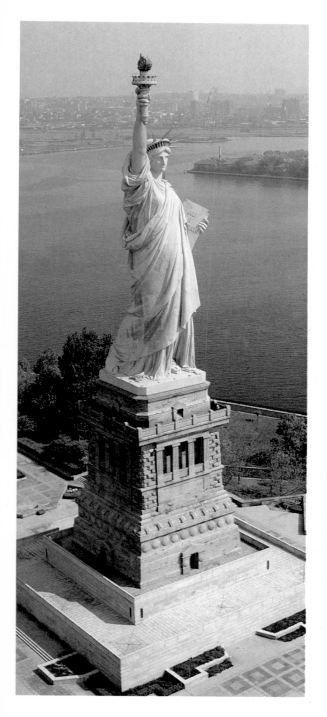

**FREDERICK-AUGUSTE
BARTHOLDI.** *Liberty
Enlightening the World.*
1884. New York.
Public works of architec-
ture or sculpture have often
become symbols of towns,
cities, and even whole
nations. It is almost always
a building or a monument
from the 19th century that
has been adopted as a symbol. The Statue of Liberty,
which the government of
the French Republic gave
to the United States of
America, is one of the most
significant of these works.
It was conceived as a modern lighthouse (with struc-
tural supports created
by Gustave Eiffel, who
designed the Eiffel Tower in
Paris), but Bartholdi's
colossal statue has become
more than a utilitarian
work—it has become a very
symbolic sculpture.

CASPAR DAVID FRIEDRICH. *Two Men Contemplating the Moon.* **1819. Gemäldegalerie, Dresden.**
Many Romantic paintings have a meaning conceived by the artist or suggested by his or her contemporaries, but the interpretation of a painting is continually changing. People have tried to find political, religious, and artistic symbolism in this painting, in which much of the expression appears through the forces of nature. The two figures— almost certainly

Romanticism was an historical attitude toward life and art in general that started at the end of the 18th century in Europe and England. It is difficult to define the term in a way that would be valid for all the works of art that could be called Romantic. The term *Romantic* was used in England as early as the 17th century. It was not until the end of the 18th century, though, that it began to be used to refer to short stories and novels of a "fantasy" nature and became a recognized term. The term would certainly not have been applied to a particular period or to a particular style if French art historians had not begun using it to compare the work of certain artists. From then on, people began to speak of a Romantic school—or at least of Romantic artists—in both literature and the visual arts.

However, there was never a concrete statement

of principles that established a starting point to separate Romanticism from other contemporary movements. Therefore, any definition of Romanticism is likely to include ambiguity and diversity. Both individual and historical aspects must be considered when defining Romantic works. Each person is a unique spectator of the world and works of art result from each individual's particular vision. "No two people have ever read the same book nor seen the same painting," said Preault, a 19th-century sculptor.

Subjectivity—an artist's personal view—is the

key to Romantic diversity. This key opens two doors. One door projects the individual into the outside world—dark, abysmal, violent, and fantastic—where nature appears to have a life of its own and the irrational is more powerful than the rational. The second door opens to a world where nature and the external world are excluded and there is a proclamation of the self, including an investigation of desires, dreams and nightmares, magic, and religious expression.

A sense of history is also fundamental to Romanticism. Romantic art embodies the realization that time is passing very quickly. It also shows a desire to recapture the past. This nostalgia was

the artist himself and a pupil—stand close together, contemplating something far from human understanding, as if they were undergoing a mystical experience.

FRANCISCO DE PAULA VAN HALEN. *The Running of the Bulls in Picturesque and Artistic Spain.*
One of the most revealing signs of Romantic feeling was the interest in cultures outside of the Western world. Anything Islamic held a particular attraction. This applies to the Romantic vision of Spain both from within and from outside its borders. Spain's dancers, fiestas, macho men, common country folk, and, above all, Spanish-Muslim monuments such as the Alhambra (palace of the Moorish kings) were constantly used as symbols of Spain. The cities of Seville and Granada helped evoke a sensual and festive world.

JENARO PEREZ VILLAAMIL. *The Castle of Gaucín.* **Museo de Bellas Artes, Granada.** *Ravines in the Alpujarras.* **Colegio de Santamarca, Madrid.**
An interest in historical styles runs parallel to the enjoyment of the architectural glories of the past. This is why medieval monuments, Islamic and Christian, are so often depicted in drawings and engravings. Such works portray a picturesque fantasy suggested by some ruin or monument. They also reveal a desire to know and to restore the ruin or monument. Villaamil, one of Spain's best landscape artists during the first half of the 19th century, painted vistas representative of the wide and theatrical Romantic "way of seeing."

the source of emotions and the basis of most art forms of the time.

Romanticism did not follow **Neoclassicism,** as some other historical movements did. Rather there was a gradual change during the first decades of the 19th century. It is difficult to know if this process of change was a conscious or an unconscious movement, if it was a response to a philosophy with stated aims or if it was simply a normal evolution. One could argue in support of either theory.

It is valid to use the term *Eclecticism* to classify most of the artistic creations of the 19th century. **Eclecticism** is not a burst of new ideas, but a blend of elements drawn from various sources. A very strong and widespread artistic movement, Eclecticism was already well known at the start of the century.

According to Eclectic philosophy, there were neither Classical nor Romantic artists. There were only good artists and bad artists, and the distinction between the two types seemed perfectly clear. Eclecticism endorsed the idea that order and progress were unchanging values—values higher than those of society and art. Eclectic artists felt that by being open to all influences they could arrive at a "happy medium" and create truth and beauty.

Traditionally, Eclecticism was not very highly esteemed. It was considered pompous, dull, superficial, false, and lacking in originality. In the middle of the century, such criticism came from the Realists—those who aspired to offer a true, impartial, and objective view of the real world, based on careful observation of contemporary life. **Realism** spread throughout Europe and America. "Let us be savage," said French novelist

WILLIAM BOUGUEREAU. *Cupid.* **c. 1895. Private Collection.**
The emergence of Realism did not result in a crisis in academic Eclecticism—at least insofar as official recognition and popularity of the artists were concerned. Eclecticism was fed basically by Raphael and Ingres. Bouguereau was the main practitioner of this style, which some critics called false and showy. In his paintings, he used religion or mythology as a theme, and his works are characterized by uniform and pearly surfaces. They also include fine details.

CONSTANTIN MEUNIER. *The Forge*. Musée d'Art, Antwerp. One of the most powerful forces of Realism was the replacement of the epics of ancient times with everyday events. Rather than portraying heroism, Realist artists tried to give dignity to common tasks. Unlike the Romantics, the Realists depicted things as they were.

Gustave Flaubert. "Let us pour strong liquor over this century of sugary water. Let us drown the bourgeoisie in strong liquor until their snouts burn and they scream with pain." Criticism of the conventional is a vital part of Realism. However, to suppose that Realism produced an exact reflection of reality is an oversimplification. Reality can never be duplicated, and an artist's perception of it is never pure.

The move toward recording contemporary life was unstoppable. Recording one instant in the contemporary world became part of the visual philosophy of **Impressionism,** the movement that succeeded Realism. Thus, Impressionism appears as the reduction of Realism to an instant, to an artist's "impression" of a precise moment. Impressionists used details to create a sensory impression rather than a social message, which was important in the works of many Realists.

FORD MADOX BROWN.
Toil. **1852-65.**
Manchester Art Gallery, Manchester.
This picture is of special interest because of its iconography and formal treatment of theme. It illustrates the elevation of manual labour, but with a touch of Symbolism. The apparent casualness of the scene is not really convincing. The painter makes it clear that setting the scene in the full summer sun was a deliberate choice and was meant to emphasize the seriousness of the content of the picture. The Realists often used a representational style that the 19th century was reluctant to abandon.

Another style that began in the middle of the 19th century is **Aestheticism.** Considered to be the opposite of Realism, Aestheticism reveals an obsessive preoccupation with beauty. Aestheticism raises beauty to the category of an end in itself, ignoring concerns for morality in art. Examples of the extreme use of the Aesthetic can be found in the castles of Ludwig II of Bavaria.

Near the end of the century, **Symbolism** was another reaction against Realism. The Symbolists were obsessed with two different subjects: sex and spirituality. They wanted to express the immaterial, the ideal, by using sensuous representations, and they exalted the mysterious.

Artists and Society in the 19th Century

Romantic artists are often described as adolescent, melancholy, and unstable. They do not "reproduce" nature, but interpret it. The Romantic artist is usually portrayed as an isolated genius.

The professional status of the artist in the 19th century depended a great deal on the official

GUSTAVE MOREAU.
The Apparition. 1874-76.
Musée Moreau, Paris.

A recurrent theme used by Symbolists is *la femme fatale*. This attraction toward woman is mixed with horror and a pleasure in self-destruction. Three typical portrayals of this theme include: woman as a vampire or as an angel of death; woman as a hybrid creature, particularly the Sphinx; and woman as a complex, gorgeous, and mysterious heroine, like Helen of Troy or Cleopatra. The superhuman Salome shown here is a dreamlike figure. She acts with indifference and irresponsibility— insensitive to whatever happens. She is shown, almost nude, before a splendid backdrop of a golden castle. She is draped in shining lace and drips with blood, balsam, and incense. John the Baptist's head, bathed in light, forces the terrified Salome to look at it, though she longs to push it away.

French Academy. That institution awarded certificates which guaranteed the professional qualifications of artists and allowed them to practise as professionals. Recognized artists could expect to occupy important social positions, practise a second profession such as teaching, and obtain state commissions (payments for specific works of art).

In the 19th century, a work of art was considered from two distinct points of view: private and public. After the French Revolution, art—as all other aspects of life—could not avoid the swings of politics. Art occupied a prominent position in a society that was undergoing sudden transformations. Never before had art, either public or private, been so subject to social ideas as during this century.

In general, two attitudes were revealed. The upper class favoured the art of Eclecticism. The working class, on the other hand, favoured the Realists, who were viewed as social reporters. The shop windows for the **fine arts** were the official salons and the independent exhibitions. Artists were subjected, as seldom before, to public opinion. Critics became primary indicators of the social structure that ruled the behaviour and even the artistic forms of the time. Juries were formed to decide which artists could exhibit their work at the official salons. These juries often became tyrannical about whose work was acceptable and whose was not. There was so much protest about the juries' decisions that independent exhibitions were formed. An example of an independent exhibition was the one established by Gustave Courbet in 1855. It was a deliberate move to argue against the officially sanctioned salons. In 1863, the official salon refused so many entrants that a "Salon des Refuses" was established to show the work of those artists whose work had been rejected. The paternalistic attitude of the state toward art began to disintegrate, and by the 1870s the Impressionists were showing in private galleries.

During the last third of the 19th century, some artists tried to reestablish the role of craftspeople in the arts, particularly by broadening the definition of art to include the decorative arts. This movement was also an attempt to interest the middle class and the rapidly expanding industries in a protest against what was considered routine and trivial.

PHILIPP OTTO RUNGE. *Self-Portrait.* **1802. Kunsthalle, Hamburg.** In this self-portrait, Runge shows himself as a young man with a strange look in his eyes and the melancholy features of someone who has probed deeply into the darkest corners of his being. In his solitude, he seems to belong to another world and to have no need to adorn himself— as happened in previous periods—with all the trappings of a society that he dared to despise. He gazes at us, slightly challenging but not quite secure— somewhat subdued by the overwhelming forces of creation.

JERÓNIMO SUÑOL. *Dante*. 1864. Museum of Modern Art, Barcelona. National fine arts exhibitions were, for many artists, a means of gaining the public acclaim that would allow them to develop their art. This work won second prize in such an exhibition. Dante, a favourite subject of the Romantics, is treated here with a serenity and solidity that recall Neo-classicism. The sculpture's simplicity is more the result of restraint than of a wish to present the theme in a new way. Spanish sculpture soon moved from this style to more ostentatious work.

TOWN PLANNING

The Industrial Revolution had sparked an undreamed-of growth of cities. It became vital to expand the narrow limits of the old city centre, to establish methods of rapid communication, and to try to balance the need for housing and the growth of the economy. The function-versus-form debate was to shape much town planning and architecture of the 19th century.

People realized that the number and placement of important buildings established a city's own special personality and was thus important from a political and prestige point of view. Socially, the 19th century city is composed of various quarters, each of which is defined within its street plan. Houses formed a part of this plan, and their facades, or fronts, gave the plan a unified appearance.

The ideas of some planners, known as "utopian urban planners," were seldom put into practice. Their plans had two things in common. First, they included new centres, or downtown areas, that would keep the benefits of the new industrialization but still offer opportunities for new social relationships. Communal living spaces were to be created in which each individual and activity formed part of an economic system, but these spaces were to be located away from all the tensions of manufacturing and commerce. Second, these plans were designed to put older buildings to new use. For example, a baroque palace served as the basis for the design of a community building.

GEORGES HAUSSMANN. *Plan of Paris.* 1853-69.
The idea of reshaping Paris arose more from a desire for publicity than from a need to practice modern town planning. Old buildings like Notre Dame and contemporary ones such as the Opera were more easily admired after the demolition of nearby housing. Boulevards and avenues were opened not only to clear up the inner city, but also to cross the whole city with splendid new arterial roads and tempt visitors into shops and theatres. In the redesign of the city, ease of access was more important than architecture, but the addition of many gardens and trees helped turn Paris into a pleasant city.

2. La ciudad posliberal   59

CHARLES FOURIER.
Plan of a Community Residence. **1822.**
This plan envisioned a single building as the home for a community of some 1,500 people of all ages. It was meant to replace the disorder and filth of miserable slums. Structurally, the building bears an extraordinary resemblance to royal Baroque palaces, an example of Fourier's wish to put the luxurious buildings of the past to new uses

Plan of the "Ring" of Vienna. **1859-72.**
A great circular road, the Ringstrasse, was built around old Vienna. The redesigned city is one of the finest combinations of 19th-century aesthetic Eclecticism and town planning. The Neoclassic parliament building, the Gothic city hall, the town theatre in Italian style, and the French-influenced university are the main buildings of Vienna that appeared on the Ring. Together with the Opera, they form a unique mixture of Classical urban tradition, 19th-century style, and the demands of the modern world.

The growth of European and American cities was governed by two opposing principles: respect for private property and the urgent need for control of sanitation and hygiene. In population, London was the largest city in 19th-century Europe. Miserable slums coexisted alongside exquisite blocks of buildings in green open

ILDEFONSO CERDÁ.
Plan for the Reform and Expansion of Barcelona.
1860.

A royal decree on 8 July 1860, gave approval for the expansion of Barcelona. In a competition the town council gave first prize to a plan for a fan-shaped expansion that used the old city as its base and had main arteries converge on it. Cerdá, whose proposal we see here, designed a network of streets parallel and vertical to the sea, on which would be superimposed two great diagonal roads. The plan showed extraordinary attention to social considerations and services and to great, wide streets. Cerdá's *General Theory of Town Planning* (1867) is one of the earliest studies of modern town plans.

spaces. Paris claimed to be the most beautiful capital in Europe, and it reflected the prestige of all of France. Certain buildings were recognized as important monuments and were the focus of avenues and tree-lined boulevards set up to cross the city. Paris was created by annexing villages and renovating the old centre. In other cities, the old historic centres were kept intact. For example, in Vienna, expansion took place around a circular road, and in Barcelona, a grid crossed by diagonals was cleverly blended with the old city.

ARCHITECTURE

CHRISTIAN JANK, EDUARD RIEDEL, and GEORG DOLLMAN. Neuschwanstein Castle. 1869-86. Bavaria.
According to legend, the mansion of the Lords of Schwanstein had once been built here. The 19th-century ruler Ludwig II re-created a feudal castle on the same site. Gigantic blocks of granite, dark fir trees, steep cliffs, and tempestuous torrents surround a building of truly theatrical showiness. The almost fairy-tale precariousness gives the castle an aesthetic yet decadent air.

Art historians have explained the evolution of 19th-century architecture as a constant interplay between the imitation of well-established forms (called **historicism,** Eclecticism, or Beaux Arts academicism) and the requirements of structure, space, and aesthetics imposed by new materials and new construction methods.

A feeling for the **picturesque** is shown in much of the architecture of the time. The picturesque is not a style but a point of view or a feeling. It should be thought of as the starting point of the architectural transformation that occurred during the 19th century. The picturesque included asymmetrical plans, a search for effects that contrasted surprisingly with nature, and, above all, exotic design. Use of these elements resulted in an emergence of forms selected from many different Western styles (particularly **Gothic**), from the Far East (India and China), or from local rustic tradition.

The interest in historical styles other than those of Greece and Italy started with the purely picturesque. Gradually, however, an interest in archaeological correctness (historicism) arose, and a true "revival" spirit was finally adopted by architects. The architect had the freedom to build according to one style or another but still comply with well-established formal rules of the past. When one speaks of Neoclassical or Neo-Gothic architecture, the reference is strictly in terms of

19

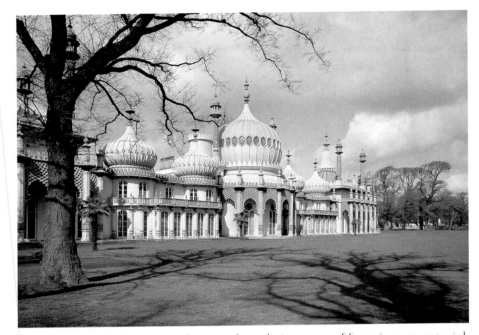

JOHN NASH. Royal Pavilion. 1815-23. Brighton.
Nash was an Eclectic who showed a sensitivity for the picturesque, as seen in this sumptuously decorated building. He produced something magical and frivolous with a capricious mixture of Chinese, Islamic, Byzantine, and Indian styles. However, the distribution and use of space within the building is strictly controlled. An important novelty was the use of cast iron as an architectural element, although it is hidden beneath the exotic exterior.

form and rarely in terms of function or material. The term *historicism* basically has only a theoretical meaning. The choice of a distinct historical style did not indicate the ultimate use to which the building would be put. For example, the Classical style was not always used just for public buildings or the Gothic just for religious buildings. Rather, the adaptation of traditional building and a new investigation into past styles were blended with a gradual use of new materials and modern requirements.

The Gothic style became particularly important during the 19th century. The first examples of Neo-Gothic architecture appeared at the end of the 18th century. Many picturesque country houses were built throughout England. Flirting with the Middle Ages was common among the Romantics. However, the rediscovery of the Gothic style carried new connotations. First, in

CHARLES BARRY and AUGUST PUGIN. Houses of Parliament. 1836-67. London.

A superficial study of the Houses of Parliament might lead one to conclude that it is a capricious and picturesque building, but only the unequal towers placed asymmetrically and its site next to the Thames River really have those characteristics. This is a building constructed in a conventional way, with two axes crossing in the centre and a tower raised over the crossing. It is a balanced and logical building, but one that is modelled after the Gothic period rather than the Neoclassical.

Germany, England, and France, Gothic architecture became identified with nationalism. Second, Gothic style became associated with religious architecture. This implied both a rediscovery of the Gothic style as an expression of medieval spiritual values and a link between form and function. It meant, too, that the Gothic style became an alternative to the Classical. As the Gothic style developed throughout the century, what could have been considered picturesque frivolities instead became academic works based on archaeology. Because the choice of Gothic as a style was sometimes dictated by the cost of the work, some distortion of historical accuracy often occurred. Gothic architecture became a well-documented system that allowed an architect to express any symbolic function.

During the second half of the 19th century, the position of Gothic style was strengthened by two

EUGÈNE-EMMANUEL VIOLLET-LE-DUC.
Illustration from
Le Dictionnaire Raisonné de l'Architecture Française. **1854-64.**
Viollet-le-Duc restored Notre Dame Cathedral in Paris, the Cluniac Abbey at Vezelay, and some of the other great French medieval monuments. In addition, he designed a number of churches, all of which show his archaeological interest. Although he was a great theoretical architect, his major reputation came from his dictionary, which provided a thorough understanding of Gothic architecture.

new and seemingly contradictory influences that linked Romantic architecture to the more functional works at the end of the century. The first of these influences was Aestheticism. John Ruskin was its main defender, and through his writings—especially *Seven Lamps of Architecture*

FRANCISCO JAREÑO.
National Library. 1865.
Madrid.
The completion of the Palace of Libraries and Museums was the most important architectural achievement in 19th-century Madrid. The building has a careful balance of academic and Eclectic elements, with a Greek facade on the second storey of the Museum of Archaeology, shown here. The plan of

the building is almost square, with two cross-shaped galleries and four very traditional courtyards.

There is also an early use of cast iron in the building. This structure presents an honest use of materials,

such as brick and stone, with no attempt to disguise or twist them to fit a chosen style.

(1849) and *The Stones of Venice* (1851-1853)—he argued that Gothic was the only style that had not been debased and degraded in the face of the new industrial civilization. He also promoted craftsmanship, emotion, and good taste rather than the products of utilitarian mass production.

Ruskin emphasized ornamental and visual values, sensitivity to materials, colours, and textures, simplicity of construction, and the integration of other art forms such as sculpture and painting. He stressed the need for additional decoration to enrich a building without hiding its basic structure. He also believed that Gothic style should be adapted to new materials and, above all, to a modern, functional approach that would form the basis of a new architecture.

The second influence on the Gothic style dealt with the techniques of building. Eugène-Emmanuel Viollet-de-Duc did the most to link Gothic methods of building to the 19th century. His use of the Gothic style on existing buildings was the real beginning of modern architecture.

Along with an interest in various Gothic styles throughout the century, the Classical styles of ancient Greece and Rome also contributed to variations of Eclecticism. One variation, called Beaux Arts Eclecticism, received its name from the fact that its practitioners came from the School of

JOSEPH PAXTON. Crystal Palace. 1850-51. London.
The first Universal Exhibition took place in London in 1851. After an international competition in which all building plans submitted were rejected, the exhibition organizers drew up their own rather conservative plans. Paxton, well known for his designs of greenhouses, then produced a set of plans that was speedily adopted. Because of his design, this building was completed quickly and at low cost. Paxton combined the new techniques of cast-iron construction (using prefabricated, mass-produced units) with a traditional treatment of decorative features and the basilica-like aspect of the building. But the real achievement was the creation of a large, well-lit space that appeared to be almost unlimited; it was marvelled at by all visitors.

Beaux Arts in Paris. This school had great prestige in both Europe and the United States during the second half of the 19th century.

The key to understanding 19th-century Eclecticism lies in recognizing that an architectural work is a combination of already-accepted styles. An architect selects and uses these styles according to technical and artistic requirements. Depending upon the imagination of the architect and the purposes of a work, the results could vary from masterpieces to the most unexpected combinations possible. Formal, symmetrical design—with regular cross sections and straight lines—often coexisted alongside more capricious and irregu-

lar design derived from the picturesque. But this practice was more common in England than in other European countries.

The history of 19th-century architecture is not just a debate about the reinterpretation of past styles. However, this was an important factor at the time, and modern art historians still find it worthy of study. Also involved were the direct consequences of the Industrial Revolution, new construction methods inspired by the use of new

HENRI LABROUSTE. Reading Room of the National Library. 1857-67. Paris.
This work is one of the first that attempted to combine the new architectural possibilities opened up by cast iron with the principles of international Eclecticism. Incorporated into a series of older buildings, the reading room achieves its functional purpose of providing a well-lit, open space. Its slender cast-iron columns support domes of **terracotta** and glass. Despite this use of modern materials, however, the room has a traditional 19th-century look. It demonstrates that new materials did not necessarily bring about a completely new style. Instead, they were incorporated into earlier, well-known architectural forms. A truly new style of architecture was yet to come.

GIUSEPPE MENGONI. Gallery of Victor Emmanuel II. 1865-75. Milan.

It has been said that today's temples—shopping malls and supermarkets, railway stations and airports—are dedicated to commerce and communications. The arcade, or covered walkway, was typical of the 19th century and is where one often finds examples of historical forms adapted to new materials and new methods of construction.

materials, and the need to respond to requirements that had never before been met.

The parts of buildings made of iron, such as columns and girders, had been used in traditional architecture since ancient times. But it was not until **cast iron** became available that it was widely used in buildings. Iron is fireproof, relatively durable, and easily shaped. Utilitarian structures such as bridges were the first in which iron was substituted completely for masonry—without any attempt to disguise the ironwork. The first such bridge in the world was opened on New Year's Day, 1781, at Ironbridge, England. By the mid-19th century, such works were considered practical engineering solutions, unconnected with "architecture." Today those works are viewed as highly important because they led to other developments. The split between engineers and architects continued throughout the century, and professionals from both areas had to be employed on a project to supply the needed technical and artistic expertise.

By the middle of the century, buildings relying entirely on load-bearing iron or steel began to appear. Most such buildings were markets, train stations, and greenhouses. Often, particularly in train stations, their external appearance was disguised to hide the real function of the building.

Around the middle of the century, a new style of cast-iron buildings emerged as the usefulness of cast iron came to be appreciated. This style was based on the possibility that a building could be erected with very slim metal columns, and it would then have a great amount of free internal space. Large exhibition halls built with cast iron reflect the taste of the century for ever-larger, ever-taller buildings. Use of the style declined after it became apparent that cast iron was not quite so durable as had once been believed.

The introduction of cast iron into Eclectic architecture posed problems, and it never became a principal building material. However, it was adapted to new needs and became integrated into functional structures.

This arcade in Milan is in the shape of a cross with an octagonal space at the intersection of the arms. One cannot help but be impressed by its size and by the heavy use of ornate detail.

GUSTAVE EIFFEL. Eiffel Tower. 1887-89. Paris. Although this tower is now considered one of the masterpieces of the 19th century, it displeased the majority of people at the time it was erected. The tower was constructed completely with prefabricated iron parts. From a strictly functional point of view, it is not a building, but from its beginning as a structure for the Universal Exhibition of 1889, it has become the most important symbol of the city of Paris. For the first time—and this is its real importance—so-called iron architecture, which had been used previously only as a hidden framework, was used in a provocative and defiant way. Cast iron was used with no attempt to disguise it.

SCULPTURE

FRANÇOIS RUDE. *The Marseillaise*. 1835-36. Paris.

This relief sculpture on the Arc de Triomphe—commonly known as *The Marseillaise*—represents volunteers departing for a 1792 war. Rivalry among artists working on the arch caused Rude's work to be restricted to this one sculpture, and it is the only one on the monument that shows inspiration and spirit. There are obvious references to Neoclassicism in the heroic nudes, but it is the enraged and explosive cry of the winged figure that transmits a more dominant expression of Romanticism. A revolutionary anthem, captured in stone, displays movement and dynamism.

There are two problems to be considered when analysing 19th-century sculpture: 1) how to identify and define the formal and thematic elements, which stemmed from the classical tradition but were influenced by 19th-century tendencies; and 2) how to recognize changes in the traditional ideas about sculpture. Historically, sculpture had always been regarded as inferior to architecture and painting. Now, however, the 19th century is seen as a golden age of sculpture.

There is a strong Romantic spirit in 19th-century sculpture. Although painters repeatedly claimed that sculpture was incapable of expressing such a spirit, sculptors tried to show that their creations were a response to the same revolutionary cry as those of painters. The sculpture of the time does exhibit a conscious Romantic feeling, and in some cases, this feeling is recognizable in theme or form. It is impossible to lay down rules for this style, to compare works, or to define time periods when Romantic sculpture flourished. Nevertheless, many artists from different countries—generally classified as Classical artists—have an undeniably Romantic point of view. It is evident in the voluptuous texture and tenderness, the complexity, and the yearning for the past that is shown in their works. Yet, in sculpture, more than in any other art form, it is clearly impossible

29

CHRISTIAN RAUCH and others. *Monument to Frederick the Great.* **1839-52. East Berlin.** Rauch is one of many sculptors unquestionably categorized as Classical. This monument is a typical example of 19th-century commemorative sculpture. This is not an isolated statue, merely dressed in the clothes of another time. Rather, it is a more complex work of art, full of symbolism and detail, and it must be appreciated in relationship to its site.

to place the various 19th-century tendencies into neat pigeonholes.

A group of French sculptors set themselves up as the standard-bearers of the Romantic cause. In opposition to the ancient ideal of beauty, they favoured the following traits: the freedom to use concrete contemporary themes; a preference for

tension and movement; a curiosity about the imperfect, even the grotesque; a renunciation of strict rules of anatomy and composition; a search for pictorial and expressive effects; and the representation of all types of emotion. These sculptors were interested in new forms of expression. Although some of the sculptors were initially rejected, all of them were eventually accepted into the artistic community and, in fact, their ideas finally triumphed. Even though these new ideas were systematically adopted by all sculptors, there was not much substantial change in sculptural imagery. Whatever their original training and intentions, these sculptors are usually called Eclectic and theirs was a period of borrowing and of blending.

ANTOINE-LOUIS BARYE. *Angelica and Roger.* **1840. The Louvre, Paris.**

This is an illustration of a scene from *Orlando Furioso*, a novel by the Italian writer Ludovico Ariosto. Roger, one of the characters, has just freed Angelica, who had been chained naked on an island. They are fleeing with the help of a dolphin that also serves as a base. This use of a theme from a novel is typical of Romantic inspiration, but the most notable element here is the power of Barye's animals, even mythological ones. He made detailed studies of animals, copied them carefully, and transmitted in his bronze sculptures the impetuousness and violence of nature, thus fusing the Romantic spirit with Naturalist detail.

HONORÉ DAUMIER.
Ratapoil. **c. 1850. Musée d'Orsay, Paris.**
Daumier was not interested in the technical problems that obsessed other sculptors of his period. Because of that, his work seems to be the most avant-garde of the century. He appears to have had a deep knowledge of, or at least a great insight into, the possibilities of sculpture, and he abandoned any attempt at representational art. The feeling of caricature in this piece—which is so similar to his drawings and paintings—gives a freshness to a matchless work of art.

In most countries there was little inclination to distinguish between the Romantic spirit found in **Classicism** and that found in Electicism. The term *Eclectic* best defines most 19th-century sculpture stylistically, because models from the past were repeated, and many stylistic stereotypes were used simultaneously. During this period, the formal values inherent in sculpture—such as the texture of the material—were often ignored in the search for scenic, narrative effects. Simplicity was avoided in favour of showing off all kinds of technical skills. The composition of 19th-century works is usually complex and full of movement, and the pieces often arouse strong emotions in the spectator—sometimes even erotic ones.

Realist sculptors were more interested in theme or subject than in formal innovation. Even if their themes were different, they are still basically considered Eclectic artists. The desire for truth in art—which was identified as dressing characters in modern clothes or portraying some aspect of daily life—had existed in France from the 1830s. This interest in genre—rustic visions of shepherds, fishers, or people in the trades—gradually widened to include the "objective" representation of all social classes, from the middle class to the manual labourers. Special mention must be made of the role of the Belgian sculptor Constantin Meunier. His representation of workers in industrial society is not picturesque. Honest toil had become a symbol of a new force.

Sculpture from the second half of the 19th century exhibits values that deserve mention. Without them, the regeneration in sculpture that happened at the turn of the century cannot be understood. One of these values was the breakdown of any distinction between worthy and unworthy subjects. All themes became acceptable. This spirit of a new reality, as seen in the work of Honoré Daumier and Jean-Baptiste Carpeaux, continued in the work of late 19th-century sculptors such as Medardo Rosso and Auguste Rodin.

Besides analysing styles and subjects, we need to consider the functional diversity of 19th-century sculpture. As in all art of the century—particularly in architecture, but in painting as well—there exists a link between form and function. Above all else, a 19th-century sculpture was required to function as an object of beauty, which means sculpture had become essentially decorative.

CONSTANTIN MEUNIER. *Dock Worker from the Port of Antwerp.* **1885. Musée National de l'Art Moderne, Paris.**
Meunier's figures show the effects of Realism on sculpture. In their solitary splendour, they appear ennobled by work, yet not pompous. It is interesting to note that by omitting such things as attention to minute detail and a pedestal, Meunier was taking the first steps toward a new appreciation of volume in a new space.

JEAN-BAPTISTE CARPEAUX. *The Dance.* **1869. Paris.**
This work was commissioned for the new Opera, which was designed by Charles Garnier. Its sensuality of movement is reminiscent of Peter-Paul Rubens, and this, coupled with the ambiguity of the central figure and the lecherous smiles of the women, suggests an orgy. The work provoked strong puritanical criticism when it first appeared.

There are two facets to this decorative aspect of 19th-century sculpture. One can be found in the technical, creative process and the traditional relationship between the artist and his or her method of working. For sculptors, this involves personal contact with their work—from a beginning sketch to carving the finished piece or creating the model from which stone or cast bronze pieces were made.

The second part of the decorative aspect is found in the essential intimacy of much 19th-century sculpture. This played a vital part in the development of portrait busts and statuettes. They conveyed various themes, which suited the taste of the middle class. The portrait bust was the most appropriate artistic subject for the Romantics. Portrait busts seemed more permanent than paintings. In busts, the careful arrangement of elements was the most important aspect: the most flattering physical features, the hair style, the dress, and, above all, the gesture depicted. Indeed, one of the annual competitions held by the School of Beaux Arts required artists to demonstrate their ability to depict various emotions in busts—pain or violence, for example.

An overview of 19th-century sculpture would be incomplete without a study of the great political and religious architectural commissions given to sculptors. Public sculptures on urban monuments and in cemeteries have left a record that demonstrates the close link between sculpture and architecture of the 19th century. We need to understand the sculptural **iconography** in relationship to buildings and monuments in order to appreciate the two arts as a whole.

RICARDO BELLVER. *The Fallen Angel.* **1876. Madrid.**
The artist won first prize with this work in the 1876 National Exhibition, and it is one of the greatest examples of 19th-century Spanish art. Bellver used a nude (depicted with clear anatomical detail) in a contorted position to portray a provocative theme. The pedestal, too, forms an important part of the whole work. Designed by the architect Francisco Jareño, it is an integral part of the sculpture, not merely a support for the figure. The whole is the result of collaboration between architect and sculptor. They decreed that the statue should stand by itself and gave precise measurements and details of what was required for its placement.

The urban monument best typifies 19th-century art: it is widespread, varied in its development, and carries many artistic and nonartistic implications. Monuments that were commissioned or were erected as part of competitions represent the values of the city dweller. They are indispensable if a city is to distinguish itself from other cities. They remind citizens of the glories of the past and of the virtues of their ancestors. In many ways, the cemetery is an idealized 19th-century city. The cemetery was often organized along the same lines as a city and was a place

JULES DALOU. *The Triumph of the Republic.* **1889. Paris.**
This monument represents the chariot of the Republic, guided by the spirit of Liberty, accompanied by figures representing Work, Justice, and Peace (or Plenty). The work was paid for by the city of Paris after a competition—even though Dalou had lost the competition for such a monument. The courtly Baroque style harks back to the times of Louis XIV in its attempt to capture the imagination of the masses.

36

ARTURO MELIDA. *Tomb of Columbus.* **1891. Seville Cathedral, Seville.**
This is a curious adaptation of an earlier tomb, but the design was altered to suit tastes at the end of the 19th century. It is repetitive and excessive, but it represents the ideals of its time. For artistic and historical knowledge, Melida had few equals in his time. In this surprising work, made of coloured bronze, he is searching for an aesthetic revival to counteract "modern bad taste."

where architecture could express itself in the wildest extremes of Eclecticism. The multitude of frozen, almost magical figures hidden away in niches and tombs gives cemeteries their sentimental and moral dimensions. There are representations of the dear departed—sometimes merely solemn and often heartbreakingly realistic. The mythical figures, such as angels and funeral symbols, seem to fuse architecture and vegetation together into a vague frontier between vanity and deification.

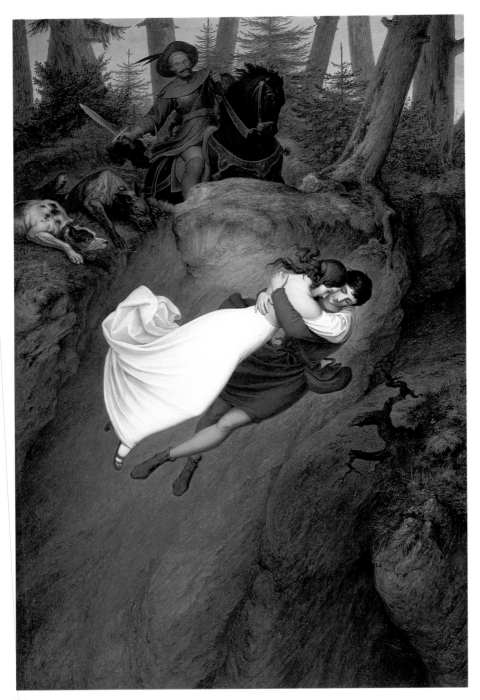

PAINTING

Throughout the 19th century, painters concerned themselves with two questions: Should artists make use of all knowledge acquired since the Renaissance and adapt it to their own time? Or, should they free painting from the traditional restraints and search for a new definition of basic concepts?

Debates on these questions took place throughout the Western world, though in different forms. Art had become international, and although Paris was often considered to be at the centre of the debate, it wasn't necessarily true that whatever was happening in Paris was also happening elsewhere. Nevertheless, Paris became the reference point for new ideas.

Romantics or Eclectics?

Romantic elements can be found in many paintings since the turn of the century. Although Théodore Géricault's *Raft of the Medusa* (1819) is considered to be the first great expression of Romanticism in painting, earlier works could well be classified as Romantic. The works of John Henry Fuseli or William Blake, for example, contain Romantic elements, such as dreamlike, angry images of the naked ego and also sublime visions of the universe.

The greatest extremes of the Romantic vision of nature—and people's attitude toward it—can be seen in the landscapes of the German artist

JOHN CONSTABLE.
Dedham Vale. **1828.
National Gallery of
Scotland, Edinburgh.**
Constable avoided stereo-
types and depicted an
emotional appreciation of
nature, as did all Roman-
tics. He planned his com-
positions carefully—the
horizon, trees, the placement of buildings, rivers,
and animals—but still
conveyed a deep, contem-
plative sensitivity to nature.
His work presents an accu-
mulation of visual experiences in which colour takes
on tonal values that are, in
turn, almost independent
of what is being depicted.

40

Caspar David Friedrich. The surroundings in his
works are distant, wide, immense, almost infi-
nite. The human being, within the composition
or without, contemplates the sublime silence of
the countryside, the deep melancholy of natural
phenomena, the mist over the mountains, the
splendour of a sunset, or the virgin snow in a win-
ter landscape. No one uses the forces of nature
better than Friedrich to express the anxieties and
incomprehension of the individual.

Filled with some of these same anxieties,
a group of German artists banded together on
10 July 1809, in Vienna. The next year they moved
to Rome and set themselves up in the Monastery
of San Isidoro. This group became known as the
Nazarenes. Their objective was to move toward a
sincere restoration of Christian art through the
use of medieval forms. They admired German and
Italian paintings of the Middle Ages and the early
Renaissance.

Their results, later converted into a teaching
system closely linked to academic tendencies,

THÉODORE GÉRICAULT. *The Raft of the Medusa.* 1819. The Louvre, Paris.

In this very significant work, Géricault is influenced by some Neoclassic techniques, but the spirit and effect of the painting are radically different. The diagonal composition and the treatment of the human forms use pictorial elements in a new and purposeful way. Géricault chose as his subject a recent shipwreck, a contemporary event. The survivors, seeing a possible rescue ship, try to attract its attention, but, unsure about being seen, they are plunged into despair. This is a Romantic painting, filled with human crises.

EUGÈNE DELACROIX. *The Death of Sardanapolus.* 1828. The Louvre, Paris.

Few works combine so many and such deeply expressed characteristics of Romantic painting. Here, form is extremely dynamic, bordering on complete disorder. The figures move with dramatic tension, and the brushstrokes of rich colour are applied freely. The theme shares this feverish movement: the dying ruler, contemplating his forthcoming death, orders an orgy. The whole atmosphere is charged with sensuality and violence—heightened by the contrast between the virility of the slaves and the voluptuousness of the harem women.

JEAN-AUGUSTE-DOMINIQUE INGRES.
The Turkish Bath.
1859-63. The Louvre, Paris.
The Source. **1820-56. Musée d'Orsay. Paris.**
Until his death in 1867, Ingres was the embodiment of most of the ideals of Neoclassicism. An idealized view of nature and drawing as the basis for all art are two of Ingres's main characteristics. His themes, however, are no different from those made fashionable by the Romantics, and promoted a method using religious narrative and a relatively primitive approach. Art historians now regard the Nazarenes as stereotyped, affected, and pretentious—the very qualities they were trying to fight against.

From the beginning of the 19th century, painting showed an increasing awareness of nature. Nature was endowed with the attributes of poetry and was skilfully portrayed—two characteristics which are important when categorizing Romanticism in paintings. Sometimes artists tried to capture the mystical poetry of the countryside and its inhabitants by presenting every detail, so minute and complete that the results tended to go beyond a mere appreciation of the scene.

John Constable and Joseph Mallord William Turner are important English landscape artists. They were the inheritors of a long British tradition of fluid, light painting and a pleasurable and respectful admiration for the countryside, trees, animals, water, sky, and clouds. Never before had in this and other ways, he is a product of his age. His Romanticism is not limited to subject matter, however. Although the discovery of the natural appeal of the nude body came from academic teaching, Ingres imbued these forms with a sensual line and soft surface. Middle-class society was prepared to tolerate—even to enjoy—these voluptuous, relaxed, carefree women, because they were placed in an exotic Oriental setting.

painting achieved such complete harmony of colour and composition with purely visual effects. The role of Constable and Turner is indispensable in understanding the changes that have taken place in modern art.

PAUL DELAROCHE.
*Execution of Lady Jane
Grey.* **1834. The National
Gallery, London.**
From the point of view of
the public and officialdom,
the most important kind of
Romantic art was historical
painting. It was common
practice to look for paral-
lels between the events of
the present and those of the
past. During the first
decades of the 19th century,
the history of England was
a popular subject among
French painters. Delaroche
repeatedly used British
themes and combined aca-
demic practice with the
characteristics of Naturalism. He was very skillful at
capturing emotions, and he
realized an exquisite precision in his exact, detailed
depictions of individual
objects. He had many imi-
tators in all countries.

In France, by the 1820s, a tendency had begun
to characterize paintings as Romantic either
by their compositions or their subjects. For
example, in the works of Pierre-Paul Prud'hon,

Théodore Géricault, and above all, Eugène Delacroix, it was possible to recognize a new school by its use of colour, turbulent compositions, brilliant brushstrokes spreading beyond the edges of the forms, and themes with exceptionally picturesque or literary character. Delacroix immediately became the standard-bearer of this movement, which opposed those who maintained the Neoclassical ideals of design. A controversy between these two attitudes was encouraged by critics who claimed to recognize

a Romantic style. But we should not read too much into this controversy. Although Romantic influences increased throughout the 19th century, we should be on our guard about viewing the ideals of that century from our own perspective.

French painters tried to combine distinctive elements from both tendencies. Thomas Couture, an ambitious and talented painter, exercised a unique role in this. He combined lessons from past masters with bold, insistent brushstrokes. His teachings spread around the world and influenced a new type of painting—one based on academic principles, but having its own original sparkle. This style became very popular during the second half of the 19th century.

THOMAS COUTURE.
The Romans of the Decadence. **1847.**
Musée d'Orsay, Paris.
This painting was one of the most famous works of art of the 19th century. Contemporaries especially valued what constituted a system of painting that could be taught and learned—a system based on famous past masters whose influence could be readily seen and understood. The ability to imitate previous great works and to combine them with a theme—both erotic and moral—appealed to the imagination of a society that revelled in exaggerated and spectacular subjects. Couture was an ambitious painter with great virtuosity, a shaper of Eclecticism, and an important teacher.

EDUARDO ROSALES.
The Testament of Isabel the Catholic. **1864. Casón, Madrid.**
Rosales played an essential role in 19th-century Spanish painting and its attempts to absorb foreign styles (especially those of France) and to produce a new interpretation of national traditions. In this work, both the formal and ideological aspects of historical painting are present. Note the emphasis on space as a cube, the attention to detail of objects, and the attitudes of the figures. Rosales's portrayal offers an obvious lesson for modern society: respect for a queen, who, even at the moment of her death, is still concerned about the destiny of the nation and shows a deep love for her people.

From Realism to Impressionism

The urge to create a vision of nature that was unhampered either by academic convention or Romantic effects grew strong in the middle of the 19th century. The origin of this Realistic representation of nature is to be found in the Barbizon school. There are as many Romantic and Classical elements in the works of the Barbizon artists as there are Naturalistic

Daubigny holds a very special place in the development of French outdoor painting. He is a direct inheritor of the experiences of the Barbizon school in depicting the natural environment without following set rules. Daubigny was especially interested in an analysis of light on objects and on the atmosphere—an interest he also managed to translate through the technique of drawing.

ones. There are also references to traditional landscapes—particularly those from 17th-century Holland and those by Nicolas Poussin and Claude Lorrain. Even though there is a romanticizing of natural elements—luxuriant trees, roads, mountains, rivers, and clouds—in contrast to previous painters, Realist artists were constantly exploring ways of transferring to canvas all the varied facets of nature. Camille Corot made a great contribution to this fusion of styles by incorporating the ideals of Classicism into the direct observation of what he saw, expressed in terms of colour and light.

CAMILLE COROT. *The Shepherd's Star.* **1864. Museum of Toulouse, Toulouse.**

Corot made a very personal and exceptional contribution to the process of realistically depicting what an artist sees. Several, sometimes contradictory, elements are involved in his work, including a balance between the unchanging and the transient, the appearance of objects in relation to the light, and the replacement of drawing with the application of large masses of colour. The vitality of his paintings and their subjects goes far beyond any idealism. All his work has an air of simplicity and serenity.

FRANZ XAVIER WINTERHALTER. *The Empress Eugenie with Her Ladies in Waiting.* **c. 1860. Chateau of Compiègne, Compiègne.**

During the latter years of the 19th century, Winterhalter was the most sought-after portrait painter among the aristocracy of Europe. His portraits have all the characteristics of Romanticism: a faithful representation of physical reality, with a tendency toward idealization; an emphasis on mood; and the use of light to create a circle that the spectator cannot penetrate. He placed his subjects in somewhat intimate poses and used technical perfection and scenic effects in a seemingly casual way. His portraits are usually superficially brilliant, but they lack creativity.

JEAN-FRANÇOIS MILLET. *The Angelus.* **1858-59. The Louvre, Paris.**

The significance of Millet's work remains ambiguous—something that happens with any artist whom we try to identify exclusively with one style. Although Millet was in contact with the Barbizon group, he was essentially a painter of ideas. Like most Romantics, he tried to express ideas through form. He did not think of nature as something that can be represented. His basic theme was peasants, whom he portrayed working or involved in some everyday activity. His use of special light, the blurring of contours, and a low horizon all alter reality, almost to the point of giving it a religious dignity and glorification. The life in Millet's canvas is real, and its subject (in spite of similarities to works of earlier painters) is revolutionary. His work always appears idyllic—the ideal 19th-century rustic paradise.

Although it is in paintings of the countryside that this move toward reality is most easily seen, other themes were equally important for the Realists. Jean-François Millet, who also was a member of the Barbizon group, painted peasants. He did the most to popularize a relatively new theme—one that moved away from the Romantic genre paintings of customs and manners, but can be definitely classified as Realist.

Another painter whose work illustrates the scope and variety of 19th-century styles is Honoré Daumier. Born in 1808, he was a contemporary of many Romantic painters. The themes he chose

HONORÉ DAUMIER.
Rue Transnonain,
15 April 1834.
Death is a recurring theme in art. The Romantics managed to transform it by justifying it in terms of love or ideals. In Realism, it appears as a trivial incident. This lithograph by Daumier was inspired by an event that happened in the reign of Louis Phillipe. During an uprising in a working-class area of Paris, a soldier was shot. In retaliation, his comrades killed all the occupants of a house. In this image of the anti-hero, of brutality and injustice, Daumier demonstrates the revolutionary possibilities of art from a political viewpoint.

(the daily life of ordinary people, people in the streets, at work, or on trains) make him appear to be a Realist. His drawings (often caricatures) and the crude satire of some of his figures attack the very basis of society. On the other hand, the emotion in his allegorical and religious works makes Daumier an artist difficult to classify. Among his contemporaries, few artists aroused such great interest.

Gustave Courbet's paintings are firmly Realist; in fact, his name became synonymous with Realism. His works best show the characteristics of that movement, although his art is obviously

MARIANO FORTUNY.
The Spanish Wedding.
**1870. Museum of Modern
Art, Barcelona.**

One current of 19th-century Spanish art that had great success in Europe was a form of Realism known as "cabinet painting." Its founder was Fortuny, whose paintings are small and generally depict 18th-century costumed scenes. In them, minor events are treated with great care and are extremely detailed. The paintings link elements of Romantic poetry with Realist innovations—broad brushstrokes and casual placement of figures within the composition.

GUSTAVE COURBET.
Burial in Ornans. **1850.**
Musée d'Orsay, Paris.
This work shows a
common event—a village
funeral. There are no recognizable people, the figures
are not arranged in any
order of importance, and
the twilight is used solely
to outline the physical
forms of the participants
and to convey the solitude
of the countryside. There is
no great drama, and the
people have no symbolic
meaning—they are depicted
as they are.

GIOVANNI FATTORI. *La Rotonda Palmieri*. 1866. Gallery of Modern Art, Florence.

Fattori is the most important artist in a group of Italian painters called the Macchiaioli. They brought together aspects of the new open-air style, like this scene on a beach. They used the most brilliant colours, ignored tone and line in favour of blurred outlines, and produced paintings based on broad areas of colour altered by light. The commonplace nature of their themes did not diminish the feeling of richness and freedom from restraint in their work. In this canvas our experience is almost exclusively one of colour and light.

influenced by past "Realist" schools, notably the Dutch and the Spanish. Courbet was a splendid revolutionary in technique, form, and iconography. This is seen in his appreciation of thick layers of paint, in the casual composition of his pictures, and in the absence of "acceptable" subjects. The content and themes of his work reject both the accepted portrayal of beauty and the presence of an ideal world. This rejection was depicted by direct representations of whatever affected modern life: work and the worker portrayed as the new, "ordinary" hero; outdoor life (beaches, picnics); town life (street scenes, cafes, dances); the family; and the woman of the world. He even depicted death as the trivial end of life as opposed to an end that had been considered glorious.

WILHELM LEIBL. *Three Women in Church*. 1878-82. Kunsthalle, Hamburg.

Leibl was a follower of Courbet, particularly in his use of colour and theme. However, unlike the French artist, the German painter Leibl executed each element in this oil painting with photographic precision and with a Naturalist's eye. He was obsessed with microscopic details and used them to raise a simple theme to a sublime level.

ÉDOUARD MANET.
Le Déjeuner sur l'Herbe.
**1863. Musée d'Orsay,
Paris.**
Manet was exceptional in
synthesizing the pictorial
ideas of past masters,
including those of his
teacher, Thomas Couture.
But Manet almost com-
pletely abandoned the tonal
gradation of colour—a fundamental of academic
teaching since the begin-
ning of the century. Instead,
he favoured the construc-
tion of a picture based
on flat planes, whose
importance he began to
realize intuitively. If any
artist sums up the division
between the past and the
present in 19th-century

Courbet's painting represented the first sudden break in the accepted concept of a work of
art. But Western painting did not follow Courbet's
guidelines exclusively, because Realist experiments were taking place all over Europe during
the second half of the 19th century. In these experiments, a relationship between light and colour
appears to have developed independently of
Courbet's strong influence. The **Pre-Raphaelites**
in England can be considered Realists because of
their declaration of sincerity, their faithfulness to
nature (instead of following academic rules), and
their treatment of themes. Yet their ideas and
works are the opposite of Courbet's, because they
have a more intellectual, escapist, and symbolic
preoccupation.

The two most important consequences of Realism were: first, a change in acceptable subject
matter—any subject was now valid, and therefore
the importance of subject matter decreased; and

second, the dissolution of what until then had been stereotyped representations of reality. No European painter or critic could fail to be influenced by these revolutionary aspects in painting even if only to be on guard against them.

Another result of the introduction of Courbet's Realism was that more and more individual styles developed, making it difficult to identify the most "authentic" Realist artists. For example, German Naturalism brought together all the clichés of the Realist spirit in its insistence on the importance of the medium and casual composition. An interesting group of painters, called the Italian art, it is Manet; his fantastic accomplishment was in synthesizing them—in bringing the elements of the past and the present together.

CLAUDE MONET. *Rouen Cathedral: Morning Effect.* **1892-94. Musée d'Orsay, Paris.**
In this painting, light and colour create a certain atmosphere. The Gothic form of the cathedral at Rouen offered Monet a perfect model for study. In less than two years he painted 20 versions of this cathedral. He was not interested in the building itself, but in the variations of atmosphere created by the changing play of colour and light on the building at different times of day.

PIERRE-AUGUSTE RENOIR. *Moulin de la Galette.* **1876. Musée d'Orsay, Paris.**
The Moulin, a small, modest dance hall in Paris, was visited by workers, students, and artists living nearby. This canvas portrays customers sitting at their tables or dancing. The sunlight falling through the leaves casts dappled shadows in various tones. Critics at the time spoke of "figures dancing on a surface resembling the violet clouds which cover the sky just before a thunderstorm."

ognizable features or from symbolic messages. This painting represents the forces of nature and the new feelings of modern people, who could travel at previously unheard-of speeds. In Turner's later works, the subject and the form became almost one in an Expressionist manner. His art has been described as the vision of a dream changed into a painting a moment before awakening.

JOSEPH MALLORD WILLIAM TURNER. *Storm at Sea.* **1840. Tate Gallery, London.**
Turner never completely managed to divorce his paintings from visible, rec-

Macchiaioli, reduced their painted surfaces to brilliant contrasts of solid areas of colour. They stressed the objective representation of the play of light on objects. This preoccupation with light, shared by many Realists, was adopted as fundamental by the French Impressionists.

The Impressionist painters, among whom were Claude Monet, Pierre-Auguste Renoir, Camille Pissarro, Edgar Degas, and the Englishman Alfred

Sisley, exhibited together between 1874 and 1886.
Each then went his own way. (Manet was a friend
of these artists and was influenced by them, but
he never exhibited with them.) Their aim was to
capture the immediate impression of a scene.
They often worked outdoors and used a rapid
and direct technique of easy flowing brushstrokes
and pure colours. In general, an Impressionist
work could be described as being preoccupied

EDGAR DEGAS. *The Glass of Absinthe.* 1876. The Louvre, Paris. *Two Blue Ballerinas.* Van der Hegolt Museum, Wuppertal.

It is said that on one occasion, a lady aggressively asked Degas why the women he painted were so ugly. "Madame," he replied, "because women usually are ugly." Whether true or not, this story illustrates one essential facet of the French avant-garde artists: the beauty of a painting is in the painting itself and not in what it represents. This attitude reveals a strong emphasis upon the formal qualities of a work as opposed to the subject matter. Degas is an exception within the Impressionist group. He preferred the human form to landscape, artificial light to natural light, drawing to patches of colour, and strange and fragmentary poses to the everyday pose—particularly if the latter carried any literary message. What he shared with the Impressionists were his palette and his technique of applying the pigment to the canvas. His images are sometimes critical and direct.

more with the value of light and atmosphere than with subject. Impressionism must be understood within the context of its time. It is tied to the history, politics, and crises of the Second Empire in France and to philosophical questions about time and space. Impressionism was also influenced by scientific and technological developments, such as new theories on colour, paint in tubes, and the explosion of a new art form—photography.

Landscapes were the Impressionists' favourite theme. Everyday subjects and events were chosen, and all were depicted according to the time of day, the natural light, and the mist or clouds present. Stylistically, the Impressionists preferred soft brushstrokes and colour and light over tight

ANTONIO MUÑOZ DEGRAIN. *Gleaners from Jericho.* **Museo de Bellas Artes, Valencia.**
The appreciation of natural and luminous qualities in painting was a general pre-occupation of late 19th-century artists, though it often took seemingly diverging roads. In a mixture of Realist and Impressionist styles, Muñoz Degrain used colours that transcend those of nature in brilliance and have an almost magical property.

draftsmanship. They sought out reflected light and its effect on colour, and they abhorred black. Impressionism is the last tenuous link between painting and the visible world as it was understood at the time; and with an almost exclusive emphasis on form, colour and light, it began the destruction of that world for painters.

Symbolists and Idealists

During the second half of the 19th century, another artistic style developed—**Symbolism.** It was an intellectual movement, thoroughly escapist, and interested in aesthetics and—as its name states—symbols. It was a direct descendant of Romanticism and showed a tendency to move away from the formalism of the academy.

In 1848, seven artists joined together in London to form the Pre-Raphaelite Brotherhood. The core of the group consisted of Dante Gabriel Rossetti, William Holman Hunt, and John Everett Millais. Their aim was to bring a new moral seriousness

PIERRE PUVIS DE CHAVANNES. *Childhood of Saint Genevieve.* **1877. Pantheon, Paris.**

The most famous works of Puvis de Chavannes are his canvas murals which he executed for various public buildings. The Third Republic undertook the task of decorating the old Pantheon with paintings in which French nationalism and religion would be linked. Many well-known painters took part in the project, which shows how Symbolism could adapt to officialdom. It distanced itself from traditional, official imagery, however, by renouncing scenic effects in favour of primitivism, simplicity, and serenity.

to painting. The members studied directly from nature and cast aside stereotyped academic rules. For five years, they sought inspiration in the works of Italian painters of the Middle Ages and the early Renaissance, as had the German Nazarenes. They worked with bright, clear colours, which gained luminosity by being applied to a white ground. Their religious and literary themes were treated in a Naturalist style. The brotherhood ended in 1862 with the death of Lizzie Siddal, Rossetti's wife, who had been a major inspiration for the group.

DANTE GABRIEL ROSSETTI. *Beata Beatrix.* **c. 1863. Tate Gallery, London.**
The curious beauty of Lizzie Siddal haunted the Pre-Raphaelites. Rossetti met her in 1850, and she posed for many works by him as well as Holman Hunt and John Everett Millais. She married Rossetti in 1860 and died two years later from a drug overdose. *Beata Beatrix*, painted after her death, is perhaps the last of Rossetti's inspired works. Heavily charged with symbolism, it reveals the ideal of womanhood that dominated the Pre-Raphaelite group—an idol, unaffected by emotion, adored solely for her irresistible presence. Rossetti depicted his wife at the moment of her death—in an ecstatic state with her head thrown back and lips parted. The haloed bird is the messenger of death, and it drops a white poppy into her hands, a symbol of passion and an allusion to the opium that killed her.

On the continent, some German painters maintained the Germanic tradition of regarding Rome and academic styles with reverence, while others exhibited a more pompous Eclecticism. Symbolism was not a major concern for them. However, in France, Symbolism found important followers who were opposed to Realism, although their work coincided with the later stages of Realist development. As in other countries, Realism appeared to be more closely linked to official circles, salons, and commissions.

Gustave Moreau was one of the key figures of the French Symbolist movement. Moreau's point of departure was Romantic. He was attracted by the fervent, colourful world of Eugène Delacroix and the sensual orientalism of Théodore Chasseriau. Although Moreau's work has a literary air (it is full of hints about beauty and love, life and death), his contribution to the pictorial field was very important. Moreau's canvasses combine sensuousness with intellectual provocation. The refined richness of his colours and the languid grace of his heroes create a curious world of their own.

Clearly distinct from the precious surfaces of Moreau are the rigidly classical compositions of Pierre Puvis de Chavannes. The most important quality of his works was the balanced structure of painted areas. His paintings, often excessively artificial because of their conventional symbolism, reside in an absolute vacuum. There is no movement, no light, no volume; and the colours are flat and lustreless. One gets the impression from his work that painting had broken with representational art, and modern painting had already been born.

DRAWINGS AND SKETCHES

**ODILON REDON:
Cactus Man. Woodner
Collection.**
Redon was one of the
strangest of the Symbolists.
Their inclination toward
the world of dreams and
the unreal became so
disquieting that the
ultimate meaning of their
work became almost
indecipherable. When
Redon's art seeks to translate a literary work into a
visual work, it is unfathom-
able. This impenetrability,
however, has its own power
and attraction and, at times,
even a touch of lyricism.

**HENRI FANTIN-
LATOUR. *Portrait of
Madame Ditte.* Woodner
Collection.**
Fantin-Latour is a singular
figure in French painting.
He is proof that, besides the
Impressionists, there were
other interesting, restless
painters experimenting
along different lines.
Although a companion of
the Impressionists, he often
used a deliberately photographic technique in his
work—an echo of lingering
traditions.

There are three important reasons for studying 19th-century drawings and sketches.
First, drawing was considered an important academic subject, both in its own right and
as a preparatory stage for a finished painting. All
students of art studied drawing as part of their
training to understand perspective, composition,
volume and space, and how these elements had
been treated by the old masters. Second, paral-
leling what we have seen in painting, we can trace
the revolution that took place and released drawing from the constrictions of conventions. The
value of nonlinear principles was recognized.

FERDINAND KHNOPFF.
Who Shall Deliver Me?
**1891. N. Manukian
Collection, Paris.**
All Symbolist works show
an almost uncontrollable
yearning for a world
beyond human experience,
a desire to express that
which lies beyond the
senses. The very term,
Symbolist, refers to something that goes beyond
physical reality. This is
depicted in painting by a
wealth of magical worlds
such as artificial landscapes
and voluptuous, exotic,
or dreamlike decorations.
The involvement with the
extrasensory world also
led to an interest in religion
and mythology, and images
of those realms are often
found in the works of
Khnopff.

Third, even though drawings and sketches have
always been of great interest to art historians (for
one thing, they show the first ideas that underlie
finished works), their value increased during the
19th century. Instead of being considered mere
preparatory studies, the brilliance and originality of sketches gave them greater importance.
Sketches became works of art in their own right.

THE ART OF REPRODUCING IMAGES

A great revolution in 19th-century art was caused by new developments in the process of printing and the subsequent ability to create multiple, identical images. Interesting in their own right, these achievements had an impact that makes them fundamentally important to the history of art as a whole.

CARLOS LUIS DE RIBERA. Cover for the magazine *El Artista*. 1834.
Illustrated magazines began to become important with the growth of the Romantic movement. *El Artista* was one of the first to print and distribute the new artistic ideas. The magazine was moderately liberal and clearly leaned toward artistic Eclecticism, which was common to the whole Romantic movement in Spain. Other periodicals that appeared during the century catered to middle-class tastes and spread and popularized a knowledge of the past and of art.

Woodcuts, which had been made since the end of the 13th century, came back into fashion during the first half of the 19th century. But it was wood engraving that became popular. The technology of papermaking was also refined. The thickness and texture of paper, for example, became more uniform. This improved the quality of the final image and facilitated the reproduction process.

In metalworking, changes also took place with the rediscovery of the art of engraving and etching. New printing presses were made of steel, and waterproof inks were developed. Above all, steel engravings made mass production of well-illustrated books a possibility.

The art of caricature formed an essential part of the critical self-consciousness of the 19th century, and its effectiveness was entirely dependent on being able to be reproduced and distributed in great numbers. In France, Honoré Daumier stands out among the caricaturists who ridiculed many aspects of the daily life of his society.

In 1796, the technique of lithography was invented, and its development had far-reaching effects. Lithography allowed artists to reproduce details of any event very rapidly. As a reproductive technique, it was easier than either wood or metal printing, and it soon became extremely valuable as a means of illustrating books.

None of the new methods of reproduction, however, could compare with photography. Although the first experimental photographs concentrated on lifeless landscapes and town views, the most frequent early use of the camera was for portraiture. Painters increasingly influenced portrait photography, especially as far as poses and backgrounds were concerned.

By far the greatest interest in photography focused on its effect on the traditional ways of representing the visible world. The invention of photography and a taste for minute descriptions of detail went hand in hand in many art forms—literature, painting, and sculpture. Many Realist painters even used photographs as an aid to capturing the appearance of their world, and this use contributed to the acceptance of the new medium. Technical improvements contributed not only to the popularity of photography, but also to the establishment of photography as an art.

Photography and painting developed a close relationship. Early photographers were strongly influenced by contemporary paintings. In a similar way, the direct and decisive nature of photography—its ability to capture detailed images—

**GUSTAVE DORÉ.
Illustration for Milton's
Paradise Lost. 1866.**
Gustave Doré, although a painter, too, was best known for his illustrations of major literary works. His training as an illustrator minimized the effect of avant-garde art on his work, which reflected already well-established stereotypes. He was extraordinarily prolific, and his work became known throughout the world. Given the nature of his work—printed illustrations—his huge output was completed with the efforts of many collaborating artists. In his images, he often reaches heights of fantastic exuberance, and reality begins to merge with dreams.

influenced painters. As the ability of photographs to capture the visible world increased, painters felt less necessity to imitate it, and they began to wrestle with other artistic questions. Simultaneously, photography showed that our vision of reality is made up not of line but of light—objects and colours are a function of light.

The ability to print from photographs also had

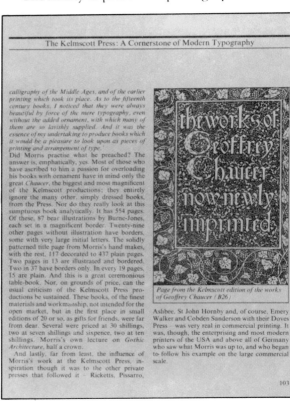

The Kelmscott Press: A Cornerstone of Modern Typography

calligraphy of the Middle Ages, and of the earlier printing which took its place. As to the fifteenth century books, I noticed that they were always beautiful by force of the mere typography, even without the added ornament, with which many of them are so lavishly supplied. And it was the essence of my undertaking to produce books which it would be a pleasure to look upon as pieces of printing and arrangement of type.
Did Morris practise what he preached? The answer is, emphatically, yes. Most of those who have ascribed to him a passion for overloading his books with ornament have in mind only the great Chaucer, the biggest and most magnificent of the Kelmscott productions; they entirely ignore the many other, simply dressed books, from the Press. Nor do they really look at this sumptuous book analytically. Of these, 87 bear illustrations by Burne-Jones, each set in a magnificent border. Twenty-nine other pages without illustration have borders, some with very large initial letters. The solidly patterned title page from Morris's hand makes, with the rest, 117 decorated to 437 plain pages. Two pages in 13 are illustrated and bordered. Two in 37 have borders only. In every 19 pages, 15 are plain. And this is a great ceremonious table-book. Nor, on grounds of price, can the usual criticism of the Kelmscott Press productions be sustained. These books, of the finest materials and workmanship, not intended for the open market, but in the first place in small editions of 20 or so, as gifts for friends, were far from dear. Several were priced at 30 shillings, two at seven shillings and sixpence, two at ten shillings. Morris's own lecture on Gothic Architecture, half a crown.
And lastly, far from least, the influence of Morris's work at the Kelmscott Press, inspiration though it was to the other private presses that followed it – Ricketts, Pissarro,

Page from the Kelmscott edition of the works of Geoffrey Chaucer (B26)

Ashbee, St John Hornby and, of course, Emery Walker and Cobden Sanderson with their Doves Press – was very real in commercial printing. It was, though, the enterprising and most modern printers of the USA and above all of Germany who saw how Morris was up to, and who began to follow his example on the large commercial scale.

103

WILLIAM MORRIS.
Illustrated page from Kelmscott Press.
Kelmscott Manor was a luxurious medieval-style mansion acquired by Morris in 1871 in partnership with the Pre-Raphaelite Rossetti. The name *Kelmscott* was given to the press, which published, among other items, love stories. The publication was carefully designed and included perfectly executed illustrations and covers. Though influenced by many older ideas, these publications shared the new interest in the art of the book and combined text and image into exquisite creations.

a great effect. Experiments in the last years of the 19th century with phototypography and photo-lithography made possible the reproduction of any natural or artistic object. That meant that for the first time, an identical image could reach thousands of people. A totally new and unexpected element in our culture had been born.

DECORATIVE ART

GEORG GILBERT SCOTT. *The Albert Memorial.* **1862-75. London.**

This is a representative work of so-called Victorian Gothic design. It was inspired by Italian Gothic, and it incorporates variations of textures and colours. The monument is perfectly integrated and has the instructive and story-telling air appropriate for such a commemorative piece.

The decorative arts flourished and proliferated during the 19th century. However, the whole debate on the role of art during that period also affected the field of decorative arts.

In general, 19th-century decorative arts demonstrate a high degree of technical skill, and—as was the case with the printed image—there was a new ability to mass-produce them. These art objects reflected the social attitudes of a new middle-class clientele and allowed novelties that were produced in many different places to become more widely known.

Ceramics maintained the traditions of past centuries. France managed to mass-produce ceramics, though with a certain loss of quality. In Sèvres, paintings were copied on porcelain, and reproductions of Italian Renaissance and Oriental ceramics were made. Exotic designs were also popular.

Technical progress in the production of glass allowed new sizes and shapes to be developed. (An example can be seen in Paxton's Crystal Palace in London, page 24.) The glass industry in Venice, Italy, found a new lease of life by copying ancient designs. France produced ornamental paperweights, decorated with flowers, insects, or geometric designs. By the second half of the century, the French were making exquisitely delicate crystal. And in Cartagena, Spain, artists continued to produce glass and white crystal.

Metalworking also flourished during the 19th century, with the development of mass-produced cast iron. There was an increased interest in new uses for iron in monuments and architecture. Decorative grilles for banks and balconies became popular. Stylistically, it was an Eclectic period for metalworking, which combined many elements borrowed from earlier Baroque and Rococo periods.

Working with gold and silver, 19th-century

WILLIAM MORRIS and PHILIP WEBB. *Saint George's Cabinet.* **1862. Victoria and Albert Museum, London.** The statement that Morris could be considered the originator of modern design might appear exaggerated. After all, the role of the craftsperson was not to resolve all the problems of design in industrial society. But through a company Morris formed, he introduced the idea that all phases of design should be coordinated. Work in stained glass, murals, wallpaper design, metal pieces, furniture, and even jewellery received the attention of specialized artists, who were trying to reestablish what they believed to be the philosophy of integrated craftsmanship.

French craftspeople made important contributions to the decorative arts. For example, Charles Christofle used the newly invented process of electroplating to make objects for the Vatican as well as a 1,200-piece set of silver tableware commissioned by Napoleon III.

In the field of textiles, older styles were copied, generally in an overly ornate fashion. Printed materials were produced that contained scenes or large floral patterns. The most interesting innovation in textiles occurred in England, where William Morris designed materials and wall coverings with an all-over floral pattern.

Despite the enormous spread of mass-produced books, the art of bookbinding was by no means lost. Many fanciful, decorative styles were used and embossed motifs often had a religious theme.

In Spain, the manufacture and use of fans has long been a strong and special interest. Romantic fans were large, with highly decorated ribs. Fans were usually covered with painted or embroidered cloth that depicted all manner of scenes. Sometimes embossed or engraved paper was also used as a covering.

By far the most interesting of the century's decorative arts was furniture making. In France, very ornate furniture—with medieval inspiration—flourished during the First Restoration. This was followed during the Second Empire by furniture designs imitating the styles of the Renaissance and the reign of Louis XV. In England, Victorian decoration is synonymous with showiness and luxury. In both countries, curious items were initially produced, and they were soon copied all over Europe. For example, there was the "confidant," an S-shaped seat, and the "indiscreet,"

LOUIS-ERNEST BARRIAS. *Nature Unveiling Herself before Science.* **1899. Musée d'Orsay, Paris.**
The use of colour is often ignored by contemporary art historians studying 19th-century architecture or sculpture. But studying the use of colour is necessary to understanding the restlessness of art at the end of the century. Barrias used natural colours, integrating stone of different colours: marble, onyx, lapis lazuli, and malachite. Here, he uses a 19th-century theme translated into carefully coloured curves that unveil the taste of a new age.

which had a place for a third person. The rocking chair, which originated in America, also became fashionable throughout Europe.

This sampling of the decorative arts demonstrates both the health and the diversity of crafts during the 19th century. Nineteenth-century testimony to the value of crafts was witnessed when, in 1851, the South Kensington Museum was founded in England. The entire museum was dedicated to the decorative arts. That date can also serve as the starting point of the battle between art and commerce. With the spread of machine-made goods—which were considered inartistic—handcrafted items were seen as the salvation of art and design. William Morris, who established the English Arts and Crafts Movement, was the main defender of this philosophy. In an attempt to eliminate what he considered cheap, mass-produced items, he founded a business of his own, which designed a wide variety of items, including furniture, wallpaper, jewellery, carpets, and glassware. Morris viewed industrial products as inartistic. He wanted to produce beautiful objects in a society that appeared eager to produce only ugly ones. His actions did not resolve the dilemma of art versus commerce, but they represent a step toward the continuation of well-designed and skilfully executed craft items.

GLOSSARY

Aestheticism: devotion to or emphasis on beauty

cast iron: a type of iron that is cast in a mould and is hard and brittle

Classicism: the style of ancient Greece and/or Rome embodied in art, architecture, and literature

droit de seigneur: customary right of a feudal lord to have sexual relations with a tenant's bride on her wedding night

Eclecticism: a blending of elements drawn from various sources

fine arts: arts concerned primarily with the the creation of beautiful objects

Gothic: a term used to describe the art and architecture of the Middle Ages (1130-1540)

historicism: a theory that emphasizes the importance of history

iconography: pictorial material that illustrates a subject; the imagery or symbolism in a work of art

Impressionism: an art style, begun in France about 1875, that replaced the traditional concept of representation of reality in painting with a new, simpler, pictorial form based on perception and executed through the interplay of light and colour; depiction of scenes, characters, or emotions by using details to evoke sensory impressions rather than to create objective reality

Neoclassicism: a movement in art, literature, music, and architecture that revived or adapted Classical style

picturesque: suggesting or resembling a picture or painted scene; charming, quaint, or vivid in appearance

Pre-Raphaelites: members of a brotherhood of artists formed in England in 1848 to restore the artistic practices of Italian art before Raphael

Realism: faithfulness in art to real life; the accurate representation of objects without idealizing them; a concern for fact or reality and rejection of the visionary

Romanticism: a literary and artistic movement that originated in the 18th century. It was characterized primarily by a rejection of Neoclassicism and an emphasis on the imagination and emotions.

subjectivity: an artist's individual view

Symbolism: an artistic movement in which objects are invested with symbolic meaning, and intangible or immaterial truths are expressed in terms of visible representation, or symbols

terra-cotta: a brownish orange clay used for statues, vases, and architectural purposes

ART THROUGHOUT THE AGES

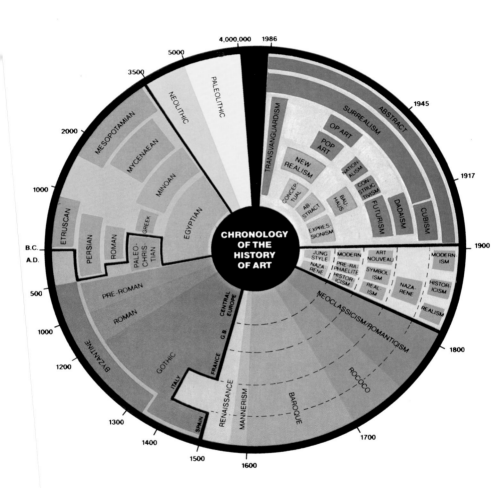

T his chart shows the evolution of Western and Near Eastern art through the ages. The terms are those that art historians traditionally use to label periods of time in various cultures where definite stylistic tendencies have occurred. The books in the Key to Art series examine the interplay of artists, ideas, methods, and cultural influences that have affected the evolution of specific art styles.

INDEX OF ILLUSTRATIONS

CONTENTS

FURTHER READING

CHIPP, Herschel, B. (Editor). *Theories of Modern Art*. University of California Press.
HITCHCOCK, H. R. *Architecture of the XIX & XX Centuries*. Penguin Books.
HONOUR, H. *Romanticism*. Penguin Books.
JANSON, H. W. *Nineteenth-century Sculpture*. Thames & Hudson.
NOVOTNY, F. *Painting and Sculpture in Europe, 1780–1880*. Penguin Books.
REWALD, J. *History of Impressionism*. Secker & Warburg.

Acknowledgments
Aisa: p. 47; A.K.G., Berlin: p. 30; A.P.: pp. 7, 15, 16 (top), 22, 24, 25, 26, 27, 33, 41, 49, 50-51, 54, 55, 47, 58, 64, 65, 66, 67, 69, 70; Bridgeman-Index: pp.9, 72; Bulloz: p. 61; Giraudon: pp. 10, 31, 32, 36, 43, 45, 47, 59, 73; I.G.D.A.: pp. 5, 6, 11, 12, 20, 41 (bottom), 42, 48 (top), 52, 53, 56, 63, 71; I.M.H., Barcelona: p. 17; National Gallery, London: p. 44; Oronoz: pp. 3, 8 (top), 13, 14, 21,23, 28,34, 35, 37, 40, 46, 50, 60; Sammlung Georg Shäfer, Euerbach: p. 38